Gentle Hands

I use my words and my gentle hands

By, Honor Alexander (Age 2)

we like to read this book daily to remind our son honor to use his words and to use his gentle hands.

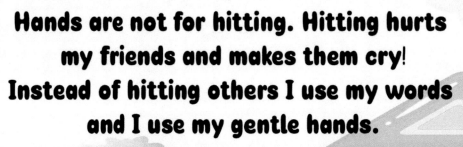

Hands are not for hitting. Hitting hurts my friends and makes them cry! Instead of hitting others I use my words and I use my gentle hands.

During playtime, I like to play with a big red fire truck. When I am done playing with the toy, I do not throw it at my friends, instead, I use my words and I say "I'm done!" and I put it away, using my gentle hands.

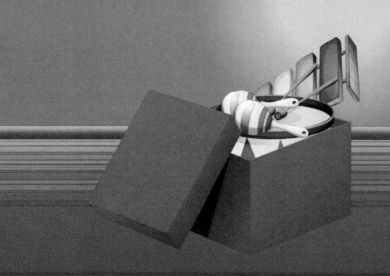

When my friends are playing all alone, and I feel jealous, and I want to play along, I use my words to ask "can I play?" and I use my gentle hands.

On the playground, everyone likes to kick the ball. It is my friends turn first and then it is my turn. Waiting is hard to do but when I want the ball, I use my words to ask "will you share pleeeeeeease?" using my gentle hands.

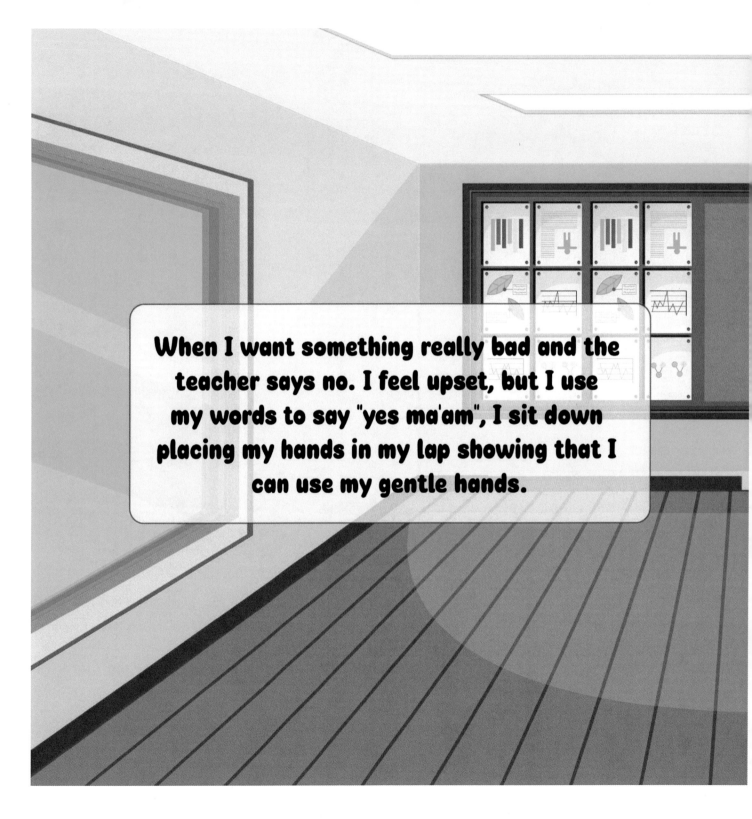

And when it is time to go to bed at night but I want to stay awake. I use my words to ask Mom to "read a book please" then I blow a kiss goodnight with my gentle hands.

Special thanks to Ms. Michelle and my other teachers for encouraging reading as an avenue to reinforce good behavior. Special thanks to Gammy and Bibi for always reminding me to use my words and gentle hands. Special thanks to Mommy and Daddy for supporting me as I grow and special thanks to Cousin Erin for her great ideas and for ensuring this book can help other kids!

Made in the USA
Las Vegas, NV
08 November 2024

11370328R00017